Class

Insecta
(Insects)

Order

Lepidoptera
*(Butterflies
and Moths)*

3%
Butterflies

97%
Moths

Family

Satyridae
(The Browns)

Speckled Wood
Wall Brown
Marbled White
Grayling
Small Heath
Hedge Brown
Mountain Ringlet etc.

Genus

Pararge

Speckled Wood

Wall Brown

Species

aegeria
*(The Speckled
Wood)*

Butterflies and moths are probably the most attractive of all the insects. Apart from a very small number, they are all quite harmless to plants and to Man.

Yet Man is responsible for many changes in the environment which have endangered some species of butterflies and moths to the point of extinction.

The felling of woodland, expansions in agriculture, building developments and road construction are killing the food plants necessary for breeding, and destroying habitats. In industrial areas some moths, e.g. the Peppered moth, have become dirty and even changed colour because of pollution in the atmosphere.

This book gives an introduction to butterflies and moths and how and where they live.

When we appreciate their beauty and develop an understanding of what is needed for their survival, perhaps some of the rarer butterflies and moths will return to our countryside.

The Joint Committee for the Conservation of British Insects has prepared a code for collectors. It is hoped that this will help to protect remaining species and some rules are printed on the inside back cover.

© LADYBIRD BOOKS LTD MCMLXXVIII

All rights reserved. No part of this publication may be reproduced, stored in a retrieval system, or transmitted in any form or by any means, electronic, mechanical, photo-copying, recording or otherwise, without the prior consent of the copyright owner.

Butterflies and Moths

written and illustrated by
John Leigh-Pemberton

Ladybird Books
Loughborough

BUTTERFLIES AND MOTHS ARE INSECTS

They form the second largest group of creatures in the animal kingdom. The biggest group are the Coleoptera or beetles which are also insects.

Mammals, reptiles, birds and fish are each made of a skeleton covered with flesh. An insect does not have this inner skeleton. Instead, it has a hard outer casing, called an *exoskeleton*, which contains the flesh.

The casing is made of *chitin*, a substance rather like our fingernails.

The bodies of butterflies and moths are much the same.

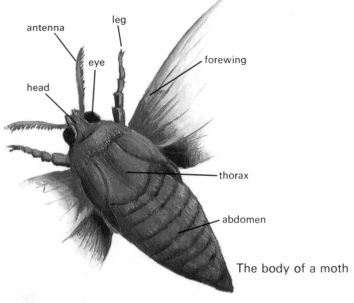

antenna

leg

eye

forewing

head

thorax

abdomen

The body of a moth

4

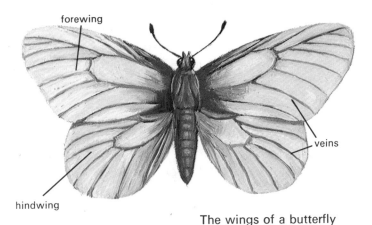

forewing

veins

hindwing

The wings of a butterfly

A butterfly's or moth's body is chiefly made up of a *head*, *thorax* (chest), and *abdomen* (stomach).

Two pairs of wings and three pairs of legs are attached to the thorax.

WINGS

There are two forewings and two hindwings.

The wings are supported by 'ribs' or 'veins'.

The wings and bodies of butterflies and moths are covered with *scales*. The scales are arranged like tiles on a roof and this makes the pattern on the wings. Some scales are filled with a *pigment* which gives them colour. Others are grooved or ridged, which gives the appearance of colour when the light is reflected off them.

SENSES

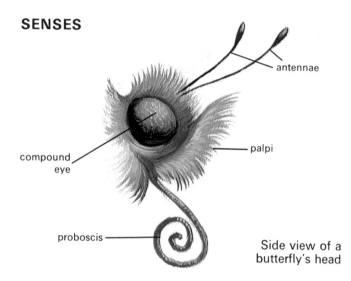

antennae

compound eye

palpi

proboscis

Side view of a butterfly's head

Butterflies have large eyes called *compound eyes*. They are made up of thousands of separate lenses which gives the butterfly a very wide angle of vision. Their eyesight is very poor but they can see movement and their eyes are sensitive to light. Both light and movement warn the butterfly of danger.

Butterflies rely mostly on their senses of smell and touch.

The hairy tufts called *palpi* are for touch and taste.

A soft pad on the end of each foot also enables the butterfly to taste.

The *antennae* or feelers of butterflies provide their sense of smell. They are also very sensitive to touch.

Butterflies can only eat liquid food because they have no chewing mouth parts.

Clouded Yellow butterfly feeding on clover

male

They mainly feed on *nectar* (a sugary juice) from flowers.

Butterflies suck this out through a feeding tube called a *proboscis*. When not in use for feeding, it curls up like a watch spring, under the head.

male

female

The Brown Argus butterfly
lays its eggs on rock rose

THE LIFE CYCLE

There are four stages in the life of a butterfly
or moth.

First there is the *egg*.

The egg hatches into a *caterpillar* or *larva*.

The caterpillar becomes the *chrysalis* or *pupa*.

From this comes the butterfly or moth. This
stage is called the *imago*.

The length of time taken at each stage varies
according to climate and temperature. In a hot
country it may only take three weeks from the
egg to the butterfly.

In this country all species hibernate for the winter
during one stage. It can take up to one year from
the egg stage to the butterfly or moth.

THE EGG

Before mating, the male and female are attracted to each other by scent. This is stimulated in glands at the base of the wing and 'smelt' by the partner through its antennae.

Butterflies lay their eggs on the leaves, stalks or flowers of plants. They choose plants upon which the young caterpillars will be able to feed. These are called food plants.

A few species lay their eggs near to the food plant and the caterpillars crawl to it to start feeding.

female

male

The White Admiral lays eggs on the leaves of honeysuckle

9

THE BIRTH OF THE CATERPILLAR

Butterflies' eggs are of many different shapes and colours.

Many kinds of butterflies lay their eggs one by one.

The egg of the Large White butterfly (much enlarged). It is the size of a pinhead

Others lay groups of eggs. Some eggs hatch in a few days while others can take many months.

As soon as they hatch, baby caterpillars start to eat. They eat all or part of their eggshells first. Then they start to feed on the food plant.

Hundreds of the young caterpillars are eaten by birds, but they have other enemies too.

Blue Tits feed
their young on
caterpillars

One of these is the ichneumon fly. It is a *parasite* (one that lives off another).

This fly lays its eggs in the bodies of caterpillars. When the fly's eggs hatch into grubs, they live on the bodies of the butterfly caterpillars. This eventually kills the caterpillars.

A few species of butterflies and moths have caterpillars which are unpleasant to taste, or poisonous. This protects them from enemies like birds.

eggs

Large White
butterfly and
baby caterpillars

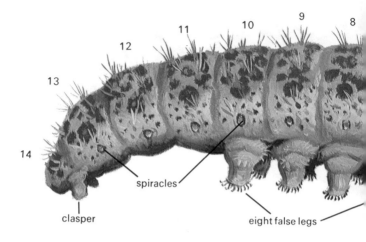

spiracles

clasper

eight false legs

THE CATERPILLAR (greatly magnified)

A caterpillar is made up of fourteen sections.

The first section is the head. Here are the powerful jaws which work sideways when the caterpillar eats.

The next three sections carry the *true legs* which are used for grasping and climbing.

The remaining sections are called *abdominal* sections and four of these have pairs of false legs called *prolegs*. These are used for walking.

Caterpillars breathe through holes called *spiracles*.

The last section has the *clasper*. This is used by

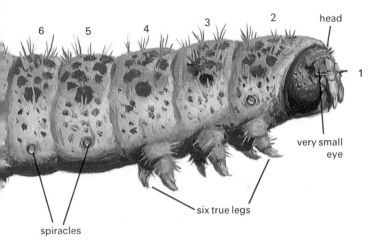

6   5   4   3   2   head

1

very small eye

six true legs

spiracles

the caterpillar to attach itself to a leaf or stem of a plant during the time it becomes a chrysalis or during a skin change.

The caterpillar's job is to feed and grow. In order to grow, it has to keep changing its skin. This is called *ecdysis*.

The skin splits behind the head and the caterpillar uses its muscles to force the old skin towards the tail until it is cast off. The caterpillar then waits several hours until the new skin and mouthparts have hardened.

The process of ecdysis usually takes place four times. The last time the caterpillar turns into a chrysalis.

THE CHRYSALIS

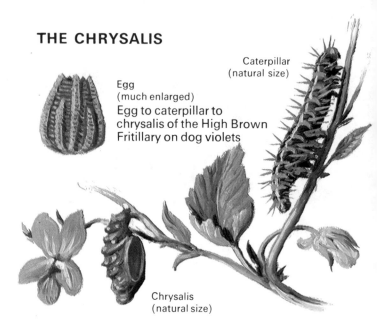

Egg
(much enlarged)
Egg to caterpillar to
chrysalis of the High Brown
Fritillary on dog violets

Caterpillar
(natural size)

Chrysalis
(natural size)

During the fourth skin change many caterpillars
spin a pad of silk from which they can hang
firmly from the stem of the food plant. Others
also spin a silk girdle round the body to support
the chrysalis.

The silk gland makes a liquid which, in the air,
hardens to become a silk thread.

The skin of the chrysalis becomes a hard shell.

Many species of butterflies will spend the cold
winter as a chrysalis.

Inside the shell, neatly folded up, is the developing
butterfly.

Chrysalis
(much enlarged)

Chrysalis comes from a Greek word meaning gold.

During this stage the wing cases, legs, proboscis, antennae and eyes of the butterfly start to form.

Later the head, thorax, abdomen, legs and wings develop.

Finally the scales on the wings are flooded with pigment which gives the wings their colour.

When the adult butterfly is ready, the chrysalis splits behind the head and the insect begins to pull itself free.

At this time the wings are very small. The butterfly crawls to a place where it can hang upside down. Liquid is pumped into the veins of the wings to stretch them to full size. It takes about an hour for the wings to become dry and firm.

male

High Brown Fritillary butterfly

COLOUR

Each kind of butterfly has its own colour and pattern. This helps the butterfly to recognise its own kind.

Many males and females of the same species are quite different in colour.

The underneath of the wings is different from

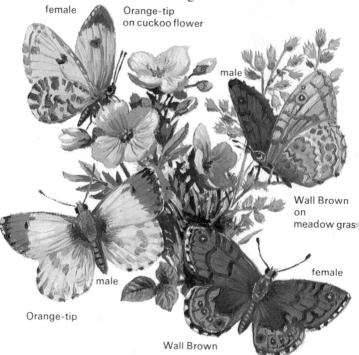

female
Orange-tip on cuckoo flower
male
Wall Brown on meadow gras
female
male
Orange-tip
Wall Brown

the topside. Butterflies often rest with their wings folded upright and the colour and pattern can help them to hide.

A butterfly can look just like the plant, branch or stone it rests on. When a creature is coloured or patterned to blend with its surroundings, this is called *camouflage*.

Some species of butterflies *mimic* (copy) the colours of one which is poisonous or bitter to taste.

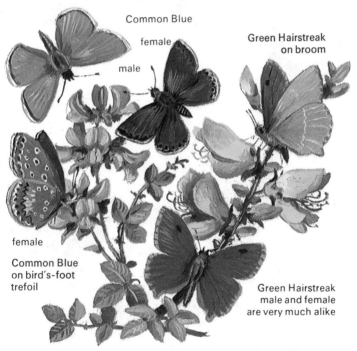

Common Blue
female
male

Green Hairstreak
on broom

female
Common Blue
on bird's-foot
trefoil

Green Hairstreak
male and female
are very much alike

This means that birds and other enemies will leave them alone because they believe them to be poisonous also.

Holly Blue

Brimstone male on buckthorn bush

male

female

GARDEN BUTTERFLIES

Some kinds of butterflies like to visit the flowers and shrubs in our gardens.

At the end of this book some plants are shown which will attract butterflies.

female

male

Small White on watercress

Small Tortoiseshell on a stinging nettle

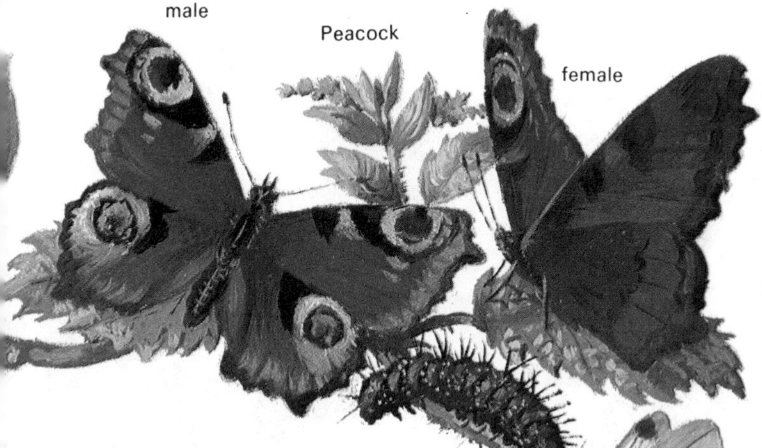

male

Peacock

female

The Holly Blue (top left) lays her
eggs among the flower heads of
holly, dogwood or ivy.

The caterpillars feed firstly on
the buds and blossom, and later
on the developing berries.

male

female

Green-veined
White on a
cuckoo
flower

Comma

Marbled White

Grizzled Skipper

Hedge Brown

female

HOW MANY KINDS?

About 20,000 species
of butterflies have
been found throughout
the world. Perhaps there are
many more yet to be discovered.

In Britain there are only about seventy kinds
but you are never likely to see this many because
some are very rare.

Changes in the environment cause numbers to
increase and decrease. One pair of butterflies
should produce just two more butterflies.

Many are lost
at each stage because
of enemies, disease
or bad conditions.
If there were no loss,
one pair of butterflies
could produce nearly
three million in one season.

Grayling

A GIANT VISITOR TO BRITAIN

The Monarch or Milkweed is a large American butterfly. Its food plant is the milkweed which gives it its name.

Because the milkweed plant is uncommon in this country, no caterpillars have ever been found here.

The Monarch is rare in Britain but every so often it may come across from America in the hold of a ship.

It has even been seen flying across the Atlantic Ocean. This butterfly can settle on a calm sea to rest, and then take off again.

The average wing span of a Monarch is ten centimetres. It is tough and leathery with a bitter taste so birds do not like to eat it.

female

Monarch or
Milkweed

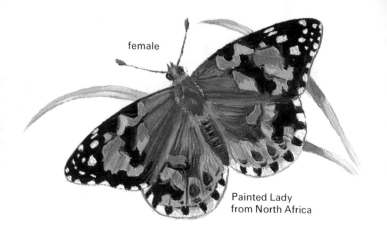

female

Painted Lady
from North Africa

MORE VISITORS FROM ABROAD (Migrants)

Other butterflies, besides the Monarch, come to
Britain as visitors. These are called *migrants*.
Every year they arrive, sometimes in large
numbers.

Although butterflies look frail, they are
powerful fliers and are often capable of flying
over wide stretches of sea.

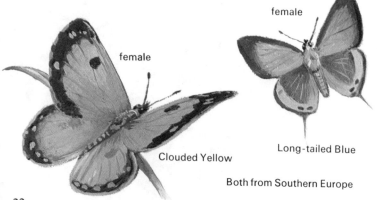

female

female

Clouded Yellow

Long-tailed Blue

Both from Southern Europe

female

Red Admiral from the Mediterranean

These are some of the butterflies which migrate to Britain from abroad.

The Camberwell Beauty (below) is rare in Britain. It comes over from Scandinavia in the timber ships.

This particular butterfly is not attracted to flowers, but feeds on oozing sap from birch trees and in the autumn, on rotting fruit.

female

Camberwell
Beauty from
Scandinavia

23

Speckled Wood on couch grass

WOODLAND BUTTERFLIES

The place where a butterfly lives is called its *habitat*.

Different kinds of butterflies choose different habitats.

This depends on what their food plant is and where it grows.

If their habitat is destroyed the butterflies will disappear.

Purple Emperor on a sallow bush

The horns on the caterpillar do not appear until after the first skinning

Ringlet
on cocksfoot

Those on these pages are some of the butterflies which like to live in woodland areas.

The Silver-washed Fritillary (below) does not lay its eggs on the food plant but in the bark of old oak trees. The caterpillars crawl to the sweet-violet on which they feed.

Silver-washed Fritillary
on sweet-violet

female

male

Meadow Brown on meadow grass

GRASS AND DOWNLAND BUTTERFLIES

Some butterflies live on grass or in downland areas. They depend on the kinds of grasses or wild flowers on which their caterpillars can feed.

When farmers make their farms bigger by ploughing the downland they are destroying the butterfly's habitat.

The Chalkhill Blue only feeds on horse-shoe vetch

male

female

female

male

Small Heath on meadow grass

Hedge cutting and the trimming of grass verges destroys the wild flowers which are food plants to these butterflies.

Many of these butterflies are becoming more rare because their habitats are being destroyed and so the caterpillars cannot feed.

The Small Copper caterpillar also likes the leaves of docks and sorrels

female

male

Small Copper on fleabane flowers

RARE BUTTERFLIES

Large Blue

Large Tortoiseshell
Found in only a few
places from Suffolk
to Hampshire

The weather in Britain is too damp and cold for most butterflies. Some kinds are very rare because, as we have seen, their habitats have been polluted or altered by Man.

Some butterflies have become scarce because they are killed by collectors. The rules at the back of this book suggest ways in which collectors can help by not killing them.

Large Copper

Once thought to be extinct,
it is now closely protected.
It has been re-introduced
at Wood Walton Fen
in Cambridgeshire.
Its caterpillars feed on great
water dock leaves and can live
through long periods under water
when the Fens flood

Swallow-tail

This is the largest native British butterfly. It is found only on the Norfolk Broads, although attempts are being made to introduce it into Cambridgeshire

A very rare butterfly which has disappeared entirely from some areas, is the Large Blue (page 28).

The caterpillars feed on the petals of wild thyme growing near an ants' nest. After the third skinning, the caterpillar finds an ant which 'milks' a honey gland on the back of the caterpillar. It is then taken by the ant down into the ants' nest, where it stays through the chrysalis stage. When the adult butterfly emerges it crawls out from the ants' nest and flies away.

This type of inter-dependent relationship with another creature is called *symbiotic*.

MOTHS

Nobody knows how many kinds of
moths there are in the world. There
may be up to one million.
97 % of the order Lepidoptera
are moths.

In Britain there are
over 2,000 kinds.

Death's Head
Hawk moth

This is the largest British moth but it is extremely
rare. It is called the Death's Head Hawk moth
because the pattern on its back looks like a
human skull.

This moth is sometimes called the Bee Tiger
because it likes honey and will enter nests for it.

It has a wing span of ten to twelve centimetres
and makes a noise like a squeaking mouse when
it is frightened.

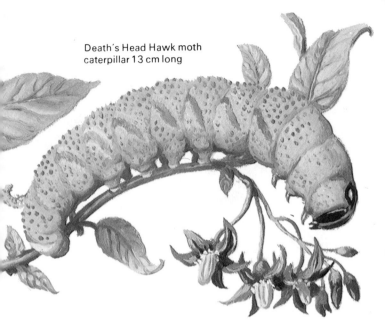

Death's Head Hawk moth
caterpillar 13 cm long

The chief difference between moths and butterflies is the shape of their antennae. The antennae of British butterflies are all of a simple club shape. Moths' antennae are of many different shapes.

Another difference which you may find easier to spot immediately is that butterflies generally rest with their wings upright. Moths mainly rest with their wings spread downwards like a sloping roof.

Butterfly

Moth

Moth

HAWK MOTHS and their caterpillars

Elephant Hawk

Most Hawk moths fly at dusk. They are built for speed with narrow wings and streamlined bodies.

Forewings are used for flying and hindwings for gliding. The body acts like a rudder for turning.

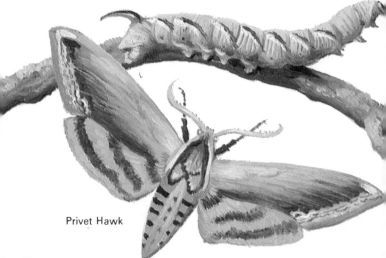

Privet Hawk

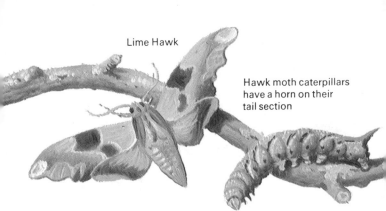

Lime Hawk

Hawk moth caterpillars have a horn on their tail section

The number of Hawk moths is limited by their food plants. A Lime Hawk moth only feeds on lime or elm trees.

The caterpillars are usually still during the day and feed at night. They bury themselves several centimetres below the ground to become chrysalises.

Poplar Hawk

Convolvulus Hawk
Its caterpillars feed
on convolvulus or
bindweed.
This moth's proboscis
is about 8 cm long

MIGRANT HAWK MOTHS

Some Hawk moths are visitors to Britain. They come to us from different parts of Europe.

The largest of these migrants is the Convolvulus Hawk. It flies at night and is attracted to sweet flowers like honeysuckle and petunias. Using its long proboscis, it can feed while flying.

Humming-bird Hawk moth
feeding in flight

Another migrant which does this is the little
Humming-bird Hawk. It flies in the day-time and
hovers as it feeds from a flower. This species of
Hawk moth, unlike others, is able to live through
the winter as an adult.

Hawk moths can beat their wings up to seventy
five times a second. They are capable of flying
at 35 mph (55 kph).

A butterfly only beats its wings about ten times
in a second.

The little Humming-bird Hawk
moth is easy to distinguish from
other Hawk moths because of
its size and its very dark
forewings which cover the
hindwings when it is resting

Buff Ermine

Ruby Tiger

Garden Tiger

Scarlet
Tiger

Garden Tiger caterpillar

THE TIGER MOTH FAMILY

The Tiger moths have no proper proboscis so they do not feed. Most moths live for only a few weeks.

The job of the adult is to lay more eggs.

Many of the Tiger moths fly by day as well as by night.

Clouded Buff
male

Clouded Buff
female

Cream Spot Tiger

Cinnabar
moth and
caterpillar

Wood Tiger

TIGER MOTH CATERPILLARS

The caterpillars of these moths are easy to recognise. They are large and furry.

The Cinnabar belongs to the same family of moths called Arctiidae. Its caterpillar is not hairy. The Cinnabar is probably the most easily seen day-flying moth.

SOME DAYTIME MOTHS

Oak Eggar

male

female

Oak Eggar
and caterpillar

Most moths come out at night but some, like these, fly by day.

Burnet moth
This type of moth is often mistaken for a butterfly.
It is small and has club-shaped antennae

Fox moth
It has feather-like antennae

male

MOTHS RESTING

Here is a moth at rest with its wings folded back along the body.

Orange Underwing resting

Moths resting during the day are quite difficult to see. This is because they are camouflaged by their wing pattern and blend with their surroundings.

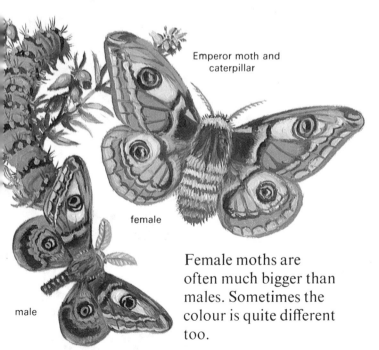

Emperor moth and caterpillar

female

male

Female moths are often much bigger than males. Sometimes the colour is quite different too.

PROTECTION

The chief enemies of moths are birds, flies, bats and hedgehogs.

Some moths protect themselves by imitating other insects.

Hornet Clearwing moth

All of the Clearwings resemble either bees, hornets or wasps. This one has transparent wings and colouring like a hornet

Bee-Hawk

A moth which is like a bumble bee

Some caterpillars have poisonous hairs. Others squirt acid.

The Brown-tail caterpillar has poisonous hairs

The Puss moth caterpillar can spray acid

THE PROMINENTS

The Puss moth belongs to a group of swift,
night-flying moths called
Prominents.

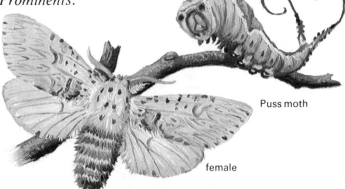

Puss moth

female

They are called Prominents because of the tufts
on their wings.

Their caterpillars unsheath two tails
like whips as a form of defence.

Lobster moth resting,
and its lobster-like
caterpillar

Prominents have very odd caterpillars.

Lace Border

Brimstone

Green Arches

Common Footman

Red Underwing

NIGHT-FLYING MOTHS

Moths which fly at night remain hidden during the day. At dusk they come out to feed on the sweet nectar of flowers.

Moths have no jaws so all their food is liquid.

Moths do not like flying when it is cold. They are attracted to lights, and even a lighthouse at sea attracts moths.

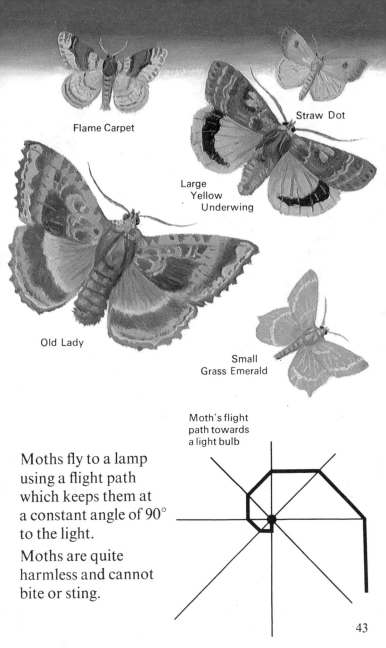

Flame Carpet

Straw Dot

Large
Yellow
Underwing

Old Lady

Small
Grass Emerald

Moth's flight
path towards
a light bulb

Moths fly to a lamp
using a flight path
which keeps them at
a constant angle of 90°
to the light.

Moths are quite
harmless and cannot
bite or sting.

43

Ear

Neglected Rustic

Chinese Character

Pretty Chalk Carpet

Rosy Footman

Foxglove Pug

Bloodvein

SOME ODD NAMES

Some moths have very odd names. A few of them are quite common, others are only found in a few places.

Carpet moths get their name from being patterned like a carpet. There are forty four

Dog's Tooth

Scarce Burnished Brass

White-spotted Pinion

Bordered Beauty

Maiden's Blush

Brussels Lace

Beautiful Snout

Purple-bordered Gold

different kinds of Carpet moths and forty six Pugs.

Brussels Lace is so named because of the lace-like pattern on its wings.

Footmen get their name from their stiff appearance when their wings are closed. There are sixteen kinds of Footmen.

THE MOTH'S COCOON

The caterpillars of moths, like those of butterflies, turn into chrysalises. Another name for the chrysalis is *pupa* (more than one would be called *pupae*).

Pupa is a Latin word which means a doll. The word puppet comes from this.

Most pupae are attached to a plant by a silken thread.

The pupa of the Lackey moth enlarged to twice its natural size

Caterpillar of a Lackey moth on an oak leaf

The silk is made by the caterpillar.

A more scientific word for caterpillar is *larva*. More than one would be called *larvae*.

The moth larva spins a web of silk round itself. Then it changes into a pupa.

To do this, the larva first shrinks,

becoming smaller and firmer. Then its skin splits behind the head and down to the tail, and falls off leaving the pupa.

At first the web and the pupa are soft but they soon harden in the air, and the pupa becomes much darker in colour.

The pupa and its web are called a *cocoon*.

Some kinds of moths bury themselves beneath the ground, and then form a cocoon.

Pupa of a
Lackey moth
attached to an
oak leaf by
its silk web

Lackey moth
It lays its eggs in bands
around stems and twigs

THE GEOMETERS

Carpets, Pugs, Waves, Thorns and Emeralds belong to a moth family called *Geometers* which means earth measurers.

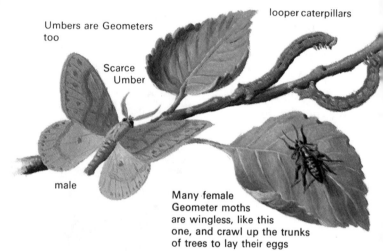

looper caterpillars

Umbers are Geometers too

Scarce Umber

male

Many female Geometer moths are wingless, like this one, and crawl up the trunks of trees to lay their eggs

Geometers take their name from the caterpillars.

Geometer caterpillars have only four claspers at the tail and no legs in the middle. They look like the twigs to which they cling.

Magpie moth
Another member of the Geometer family

Common Emerald

Geometer caterpillars move by making a series of loops. This is why they are known as *loopers*. They are also sometimes called inch worms. The adults are often small and like butterflies at first glance.

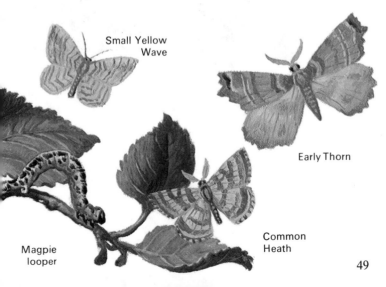

Small Yellow Wave

Early Thorn

Common Heath

Magpie looper

49

lilac

helenium

phlox

rock rose

cornflow

sweet
william

primrose

Michaelmas daisy

FLOWERS FOR BUTTERFLIES

If you have a garden you can attract butterflies
and moths to it.

Here are some of the flowers you could plant
for them. Many can be grown from seeds.

Butterflies like sweet flowers. They seem to like
purple and yellow flowers best.

buddleia

arabis

tobacco
plant

thrift

wallflower

scabious

ox-eye
daisy

Butterflies do not visit roses or showy flowers
like lilies but they like simple flowers and weeds.

This is why we must be careful not to kill the
hedgerows and wild flowers of the countryside.

INDEX OF BUTTERFLIES AND MOTHS